# MOUAT'S
## The First Hundred Years

*Dedicated to Ivan Mouat and Manson Toynbee – cousins who loved Salt Spring and who loved Mouat's*

# MOUAT'S
## The First Hundred Years

Charles Kahn

Mouat's Trading Company

# Preface

From its inception, Mouat's has been a family business. It all started in 1907, when Gilbert Mouat and his mother, Jane, bought an existing general store in Ganges, calling it G. J. Mouat and Company. After Gilbert's brother William Manson joined the company, the name changed to Mouat Brothers Company Limited. When Gilbert died, his sons – Laurie, Colin, and Mac – took over the management of the company. Then in 1969, the company was sold to a group headed by Dick, Tom, and Manson Toynbee, the sons of Jessie Toynbee (née Mouat) and grandsons of Jane Mouat. Since 2000, a new consortium led by Kevin Bell, Dick Toynbee's son-in-law, bought the company, so the family connection continues into the firm's second century.

One hundred years after its founding, Mouat's still retains many of the same characteristics that it had in its youth. While the original store had almost everything under one roof and supplied almost all of Salt Spring Islanders' needs, the company today is more specialized and operates from several different locations and as several different business entities:

- Mouat's main store is really three stores in one: Bed, Bath, and Homeware upstairs, Home Hardware on the main floor, and The Housewares Store in the basement.

- Mouat's Clothing, in the Harbour Building, is a destination store that attracts customers throughout the Pacific Northwest.

- Old Salty, also in the Harbour Building, sells a variety of merchandise, including greeting cards, wrapping paper, newspapers and magazines, and gift, gourmet, and souvenir items.

Today, as in the past, Mouat's is downtown Ganges' largest commercial landowner, renting space to a wide variety of businesses in eleven separate buildings. In many ways, Mouat's has shaped Ganges over the years, developing an island centre that serves residents and tourists alike. To celebrate its centenary, the company is proud to share the background and story of this accomplishment.

# Abbreviated Family Tree of Store Ownership

Almost every member of the Mouat family was involved in the family business at some time, if only with summer jobs as students. Since the family is very large, it is impossible to represent everyone here. Thus, the following family tree contains only those Mouats and Toynbees who worked in the company for many years and were part of the store's ownership. Whenever you are confused about one of the people mentioned in the following pages, refer to this little family map.

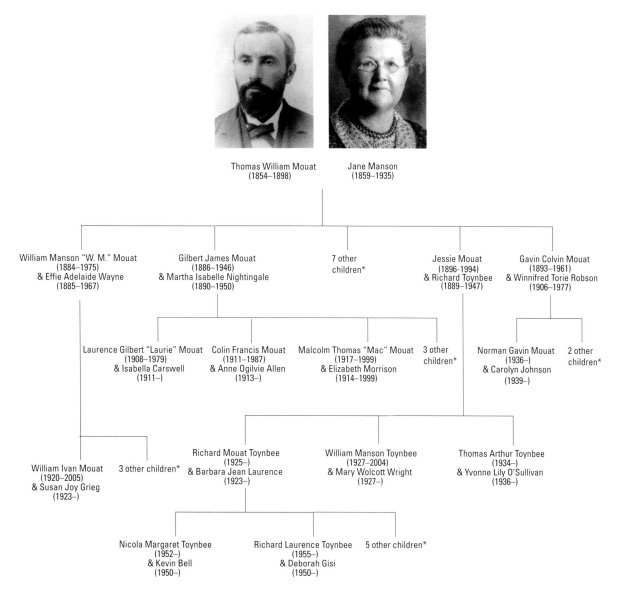

Thomas William Mouat
(1854–1898)

Jane Manson
(1859–1935)

William Manson "W. M." Mouat
(1884–1975)
& Effie Adelaide Wayne
(1885–1967)

Gilbert James Mouat
(1886–1946)
& Martha Isabelle Nightingale
(1890–1950)

7 other
children*

Jessie Mouat
(1896-1994)
& Richard Toynbee
(1889–1947)

Gavin Colvin Mouat
(1893–1961)
& Winnifred Torie Robson
(1906–1977)

Laurence Gilbert "Laurie" Mouat
(1908–1979)
& Isabella Carswell
(1911–)

Colin Francis Mouat
(1911–1987)
& Anne Ogilvie Allen
(1913–)

Malcolm Thomas "Mac" Mouat
(1917–1999)
& Elizabeth Morrison
(1914–1999)

3 other
children*

Norman Gavin Mouat
(1936–)
& Carolyn Johnson
(1939–)

2 other
children*

William Ivan Mouat
(1920–2005)
& Susan Joy Grieg
(1923–)

3 other children*

Richard Mouat Toynbee
(1925–)
& Barbara Jean Laurence
(1923–)

William Manson Toynbee
(1927–2004)
& Mary Wolcott Wright
(1927–)

Thomas Arthur Toynbee
(1934–)
& Yvonne Lily O'Sullivan
(1936–)

Nicola Margaret Toynbee
(1952–)
& Kevin Bell
(1950–)

Richard Laurence Toynbee
(1955–)
& Deborah Gisi
(1950–)

5 other children*

*siblings not involved in the family business

# In the Beginning, 1907–1946

Mouat's was built on a solid foundation established by another Salt Spring pioneer family. In 1900, Joel Broadwell opened his second store at Central. A year later, he sold it to two cousins – Joe Malcolm, a blacksmith, and Percy Purvis, who had both arrived on the island from Ontario in 1889.

In 1904, Malcolm and Purvis moved the store to Ganges, where they built sheds and a blacksmith shop at the end of the Ganges wharf. From here they operated an export business using two boats, the 30-foot *Nomad* and, later, the 60-foot *Ganges*. The only competition was a store on Ganges Hill, operated since 1900 by Abraham Reid Bittancourt.

In 1907, after the sudden death of Joe Malcolm, Jane Mouat and her son Gilbert James, who had been

**Malcolm and Purvis's store, c. 1905.** Boat day in Ganges brought settlers down to the store to pick up their mail and supplies. The store in the background is the one purchased by the Mouats in 1907. Note the oxen that some islanders used instead of horses.

**G. J. Mouat and Company staff on the porch of the recently acquired store in about 1907.** *From left to right:* Jim Rogers, Bill Akerman, Will (W. M.) Mouat, Douglas Harris, Gilbert Mouat, and Gavin Mouat. Fred Crofton, who wasn't an employee, is on the far right.

working for Malcolm and Purvis, bought the business, renaming it G. J. Mouat and Company. Jane had to mortgage the family farm to raise the money to buy the business. Gilbert managed most of the store's day-to-day business, while Jane took care of the post office.

**The original seaside village.** This photo shows how much early Ganges was oriented to the water. Coastal steamers like the *Joan* and later the *Princess Mary* docked on the outside near the shed originally built by Malcolm and Purvis. The other docks could accommodate the company's two boats as well as those of customers, who were as likely to come by water as by land.

In 1909, Gilbert's brother Will (or W. M. as he was later called) joined the firm. W. M. had been studying at Columbia College and wanted to be a lawyer, but his life took another turn. Instead, he left university and returned home to join the firm as a third partner, and on June 30, 1910, the company was incorporated as Mouat Brothers Company Limited. A few years later, the youngest Mouat brother, Gavin, joined the firm.

**A new sign for a new partnership.**
The company name now reflects the addition of W. M. When the current building was constructed in 1912, the original store (shown here) continued to be used as Granny's Boarding House, which was run by Jane Mouat. It became the home of some family members, as well as a boarding house for store employees. Later as the Ganges Inn, it served travellers as well as islanders, such as high-school student Lotus Fraser (Ruckle) who stayed there on weekdays to avoid the long daily trip from Beaver Point to Ganges. Lotus worked for Granny Mouat to pay for her board. This building no longer exists.

# The Family Origins

Thomas William Mouat and his wife Jane emigrated from the Shetland Islands in 1884 to Nanaimo, but left that city the next year. On Joel Broadwell's recommendation, they bought Abraham Copeland's farm on what is now Tripp Road on St. Mary Lake.

The Mouats were very happy on Salt Spring. In an 1895 publication, the Rev. E. F. Wilson quoted Thomas Mouat as follows: "I consider my farm of more value to me than a salary of $80 or $85 a month in the city. My poultry alone pay their own cost and find us in flour and groceries, which is pretty well for a family of ten. Poultry raising and dairying I consider to be the most profitable line. We have Jersey cows and Leghorn and Spanish fowls."

Farm life demanded long hours of hard work, particularly for Thomas Mouat, whose health was poor. When he died in 1898 at forty-five, he left Jane with eleven children: Thomas William – a son from his first marriage to Mary Manson – and ten children from his marriage to Jane – Margaret Janet, William Manson, Gilbert James, Mary Jane, Laurence, Lydia, Gavin Colvin, Jeremiah, Jessie, and Grace. The older children were a great help on the farm.

**The original Mouat farmhouse on Tripp Road by St. Mary Lake.** The people who currently live in the Mouat home continue to farm on part of the original Mouat farmland.

The store was soon essential to island life. Not only did it provide islanders with their basic supplies, but it bought much of the produce of the island's farmers, who often referred to themselves as "ranchers." This produce included sheep, calves, pigs, the occasional cow, eggs, and fruit. Milk and cream were about the only produce the store didn't buy, as these went to the local creamery instead. Farmers often exchanged their produce for store-bought goods. This saved them the cost of transporting their goods to the city and also ensured that the farmers were able to pay Mouat's for their purchases.

**Jane Mouat and eight of her children, c. 1908.** *Left to right and back to front:* Jerry, Laurie, William (W. M.), Gilbert, Gavin, Mary, Mrs. Jane Mouat, Lydia, and Jessie *(in front).* The reason everyone looks so sad in this photo is because the family was about to leave the farm on St. Mary Lake.

**Gilbert James Mouat with his wife, Belle, c. 1931.** Gilbert was the fourth child of Thomas and Jane Mouat. He started working for Malcolm and Purvis when he was still a teenager. He married Martha Isabelle (Belle) Nightingale, a granddaughter of Salt Spring pioneers Martha and Joseph Akerman, in 1908. Both Gilbert and Belle were very active in the community. For example, Belle was one of the founding members and a president of the Lady Minto Hospital Auxiliary.

## A Fair But Exacting Boss

Everyone liked Gilbert Mouat as a boss, but he did expect his employees to work hard for him. Ivan Mouat remembered that he didn't like it if people weren't hard at work. Even when there was nothing important to do, employees would grab a feather duster and start dusting when they saw Gilbert approaching.

Gilbert was a very dynamic person. Here's how Edward Cartwright, who worked with Gilbert at Malcolm and Purvis's store, assessed young Gilbert in his book *A Late Summer: The Memoirs of E. R. Cartwright*:

> Along with Malcolm and Purvis at the store there worked one Gilbert Mouat, quite young but of outstanding ability. He saw all the possibilities and threw himself heart and soul into it. Many days and nights he and I spent together on the *Nomad* working our way up to Ladysmith and back – generally nights, as the preparation and loading of the cargo was done by day, and Purvis was much too keen a business man to let the boat be idle all night. In no time I came to see that Gilbert, although much younger, was a born salesman and had the better brain of the two. It was not many years before he and his brother took over the business, store and all. The last time I saw him was in 1925 when I stayed with the Will Scotts for a few days. Polio had dealt him a cruel blow and he was in a wheelchair, but the charm, the brain and the courage were still there, and it was plain to see that he and his family owned and ran a very real business.

The company did so well under Gilbert and W. M. that it was able to purchase Reid Bittancourt's business for only the goodwill in 1910 and, two years later, to build a new building for the store right next door to the old building. When this store (the building still

Malcolm and Purvis always had a barrel of cider on tap, which they sold for five cents a glass. The day Jane Mouat and her son Gilbert bought the store, the barrel went out the door. Granny was a strict Methodist and liquor wasn't part of her life.

**The original G. J. Mouat and Company store on the left and the 1912 version with its new name – Mouat Bros. Co. Ltd. – on the right.** The original store was where the Purvis Building is today (occupied by Glad's Ice Cream and Sweet Shoppe and West of the Moon). The 1912 building and the Purvis Building are now separated by a road.

occupied by Mouat's hardware and housewares today) was built, the original store became a boarding house, which soon became known as "Granny's Boarding House" because it was run by Jane Mouat. Later on, it was called the Ganges Inn. Store employees, members of the Mouat family, and travelling salesmen lived there, as did Jane Mouat herself until her death in 1935.

Gilbert and W. M. worked very hard to develop the new business, but Gilbert was forced to the sidelines when he developed polio in 1914. He was hospitalized for an extended period and then went to Vancouver for further treatment. For two years, Gilbert fought the illness, while his brother W. M. and his mother, Jane, ran the business. Gilbert never regained the use of his legs. When he was finally able to return to manage the store, a manual elevator was installed to get him to his second-floor office. (The boxlike object on the roof of Mouat's store in the photo on page 38 is all that remained of the elevator after it was removed in the late-1940s following Gilbert's death.)

**Sixteen-year-old Jessie Mouat (later Toynbee) poses in the window of Mouat's partially completed new building in 1912.**

Later on, Gilbert regularly cruised along the upper perimeter walkway in his wheelchair to check on what was happening downstairs. If things were not to his satisfaction, he'd send a note to anyone who was on duty downstairs via the electrical carrier system installed in 1937 when electricity came to the north end of the island. Prior to that time, the store used kerosene lighting and then a "wet cell" electric generating system for power.

The business was a very important part of Gilbert's life, and he expanded it in several ways. According to his daughter Peggy Johnston:

**Interior of Mouat Bros. (c. 1912).** According to Gilbert's wife, Belle, "This is a view of the sporting goods and hardware counter. This is just as you come in the front door on the right hand. You will go some to find a section in a city store that looks better than this."

He was a keen businessman and his time at work frequently involved his social life. He never put business ahead of friendship or of his concern for someone else's needs. This latter characteristic could well have posed a threat to the financial state of the business over the years without the watchful eye of his older brother, Will [W. M.]. They had a firm partnership and were truly dependent on each other's performance … forming a good basis for a solid business.

MOUAT'S: THE FIRST HUNDRED YEARS

**The centre of the first floor of Mouat's.** According to Belle Mouat, "This is a view of the centre of the first floor of our store showing the stairs with the paint and oil department at the top of the stairs. You will see the window. That window is used for displaying shoes."

Gilbert was also the local notary public and spent a good deal of time advising and helping people who came to see him. From the 1920s, in addition to his office hours, Gilbert conducted business from home in the evenings or early mornings using the island's quickly expanding telephone service. This business included scaling and selling logs, buying lumber, shipping dressed cattle or lambs to meat wholesalers, checking invoices and packing slips, and at times making funeral arrangements for an islander who had died. In the early days, these arrangements were carried out by Allan Cartwright, a store employee.

**Ford Rally, c. 1914.** This popular rally brought out many islanders and no doubt helped Mouat's sell its cars. In the photo above, that's W. M. at the wheel and Gavin on the right. In the photo to the right, Ernest and Mary Crofton and Mary's brother, Harry Bullock, are in the first car, and Dr. Allen Beech, Mrs. Beech, and Gavin Mouat (the driver) are in the second car.

Gilbert's importance and prominence on Salt Spring until his death in 1946 cannot be overstated. Charlie Horel was one of his many admirers:

> Gilbert Mouat was the patriarch of Salt Spring. He became in effect all things to all men. He handed out lumber orders, he handled financing – all forms of power ran through Gilbert Mouat's hands. Very few men in that position would have handled that type of power as tolerantly and decently as Mouat did.

Mouat Brothers sold everything required for the farm or home: hardware, groceries, meats, produce, feed grains, lumber, dry goods, and petroleum products. In 1914, it acquired a Ford dealership and soon had a garage to service the vehicles it sold.

Here's how Charlie Horel remembered Mouat's close to fifty years later:

> G. J. Mouat was the head of the largest business on the Island, Mouat Brothers Ltd., a general store that was really more of a community emporium than a store. You could buy groceries and shoe polish, horse harness and blacksmith tools, blankets and furniture or a cemetery lot or a farm complete with stock – everything was available at Mouat Brothers. In addition, G. J. bought and sold logs and poles and piling, and he financed the loggers while they were getting their timber ready. Mouat Brothers also sold hunting and fishing licences, registered births and deaths, and bought and graded eggs from the local farmers, as well as beef, lamb and fowl. You see, you could hardly draw breath on Salt Spring Island without getting involved with Mouat Brothers Ltd.

**The original store on the left and the new store on the right.** Back then, there wasn't much in Ganges besides Mouat's.

MOUAT'S: THE FIRST HUNDRED YEARS

The Mutual Life
ASSURANCE Co. OF CANADA

ESTABLISHED 1869

HOME OFFICE
WATERLOO, ONT.

202 TIMES BUILDING
VICTORIA, B. C.

H F Shade
AGENT

March 30 - 1926

Mouat Bros
Ganges

Gentlemen:— Will you please deliver to
my cabin at Cretton Lake, the
appended list of provisions overleaf —
together with the bill for same —
not later than ~~Saturday~~ Thursday noon ~~night~~. Sure

Mowat Bros have a reputation
of never disappointing a fisherman
so please be sure and have this
delivered for sure

Yours faithfully,

Herbert F Slade

# The Competition

Despite his usual business acumen, Gilbert didn't always do everything right. Two stories about the founding of the Salt Spring Island Trading Company, a Mouat competitor for many years, attribute that company's founding to Gilbert's individualistic approach to business. Here's the first version from a 1975 interview with John Charles Lang's daughters:

> In 1912, John Charles Lang, a retired but still energetic railway construction engineer, entered Mouat's, found the article he wanted, and asked its price. Unsure, Walter Norton, the clerk, called up to Gilbert's office where the president was sitting in his wheelchair. "What does this cost?" "Who's it for?" was the response, at which point Lang decided that it was about time that Mouat's had some competition.

**Salt Spring Island Trading Company, c. 1930**

According to this story, Lang joined with others who shared his love of competition – Will, Frank, and Geoff Scott, Harry Bullock, and T. F. Speed – and launched the Salt Spring Island Trading Company.

The second version of the Salt Spring Island Trading Company's beginning was provided by Ivan Mouat:

> Gilbert Mouat was helping Hiram Whims carry his purchases out to his wagon. Meanwhile, Harry Bullock, the self-styled "Squire of Salt Spring Island," pulled up in his gig, calling "Gilbert!" Gilbert answered, "Just a minute, Mr. Bullock," and made another trip to the wagon. Again Bullock called, somewhat irately, "Gilbert!" But Gilbert concentrated on loading Whims's wagon. "Gilbert, in England when the squire of the village drives up, the shopkeeper comes out and takes his order." "Well, Mr. Bullock, this isn't England, and I didn't think you were the squire, so you will just have to come in like everybody else and get your order."

The inside of the Salt Spring Island Trading Company, c. 1940. That's Stanley Wagg on the ladder. He worked in the store for forty-six years from the time he arrived on Salt Spring in 1921. Wagg became the store manager in 1945.

According to Ivan, Bullock then started the Salt Spring Island Trading Company. Its first manager, Douglas Harris, had been a Mouat's employee.

The Trading Company handled mainly groceries and feed, so it wasn't a major competitor for Mouat's. However, Woodward's in Vancouver and David Spencer's store in Victoria certainly were. Mouat's couldn't compete with the lower prices made possible by the larger buying power of these mail-order emporiums, and this was a constant thorn in Gilbert's side. He spent a great deal of time pointing out to anyone who'd listen that islanders should shop at Mouat's because, by the time they paid the freight to obtain cheaper goods from off-island, Mouat's prices were competitive. It's interesting to note that many department stores, including Woodward's and David Spencer's, are no longer in business, while Mouat's still is, largely because it responded effectively to changes in the marketplace.

**Malcolm and Purvis family picnic, c. 1904.** Picnics were a tradition continued from the Malcolm and Purvis days. *Rear, left to right:* Joe Malcolm, Margaret Malcolm, Mary Mouat, W. M. Mouat, Percy Purvis, Gilbert Mouat, W. H. McAfee; *middle:* Laurie Mouat, Bill Purvis, Ethel Purvis, Jane Mouat, Jessie Mouat, Beth Purvis, Susan Purvis holding Jack; *front:* Jerry Mouat, Lydia Mouat, Belle Nightingale, Herbert Purvis, Margaret (Minnie) Mouat, Jean Purvis, Eva Jenkins. Note that Belle Nightingale later became Gilbert's wife and that the Laurie Mouat shown here is Gilbert's younger brother who died in 1909 and not his son of the same name.

## A Friendly Place to Work

According to all reports, Mouat's has always been a good place to work, where people have fun on and off the job and management and staff join together to celebrate the summer with picnics, and Christmas and other special occasions with parties. Anne Mouat remembered that everyone involved with the company would gather at the Ganges Inn for Christmas dinner, which in the early days was cooked by Jane Mouat herself. Ian Brown, Mouat's manager in the 1970s and 1980s, remembered, "We had a good staff, who in turn, enjoyed working for the company. The Toynbees provided annual picnics, golf tournaments, bowling parties, etc. We were just like a big happy family!"

**Granny's Boarding House, c. 1910.**
Once the original store started by Malcolm and Purvis, the building continued as Granny's Boarding House run by Jane Mouat. Store employees often enjoyed meals served by Jane herself. Everyone in the store came to the Boarding House for Christmas dinner.

**Gilbert, W. M., Gavin, and Mouat's staff in about 1926.**
*Rear:* Tom Liversitch, Alan Cartwright (lumber, trucking, undertaking), Ken Butterfield (bookkeeper), Fred Wagg, Gerald Ringwood (postal clerk), Arthur Meacock, Bill Page (manager of the feed shed), Walter Norton, Fred Stacey, Arthur Elliot, Laurie Mouat, and Herbert Kingdom. *Sitting:* Gavin Mouat, Zan Rogers, Margaret (Aunt Maggie) Manson, and W. M. Mouat. *Front:* Colin Mouat, Gilbert Mouat, and Oliver Mouat. Aunt Maggie Manson, who was Jane Mouat's sister, ran the dry-goods department.

# Mouat's in the Thirties and Forties

**Long-time islander Bob Rush reminisced about the Mouat's he remembered from the 1930s and 1940s:**

> From my perspective as a kid at the time, I considered Mouat's store to be the centre of the universe. It was the main commercial centre of the island, and on the three days a week that the CPR steamer came in, it was also the social centre.
>
> Mouat's provided a wide range of goods and services. Inside they sold groceries, hardware, work clothes, dry goods, shoes, sporting goods, guns, ammunition, fishing tackle, stationery. They sold insurance and real estate. They also brought in sacks of feed for the numerous chicken, cattle, and other farming operations on the island.
>
> They had the Ford car dealership and a repair garage across the way. They had a gas pump out in front. They were also the dealer for Imperial Oil and sold oil from bulk tanks. You name it, they had it, or they'd bring it in for you!

**Mouat's, c. 1942.** The Imperial Oil sign indicates where the gas pump was located between the store and the feed and storage shed.

**Arthur John "Pop" Eaton.** From 1923 to 1928, Pop Eaton was the postmaster in Fulford. Pop also ran the White House Hotel, a predecessor of the Fulford Inn, and for a few years the post office was housed there. Following the death of Jane Mouat in 1935, and until 1964, he was the postmaster in the Ganges Post Office located in Mouat's.

Pop Eaton was also an island character. He was known as a fine entertainer, playing in dance bands in both south and north Salt Spring. When he wasn't playing for others, he enjoyed dancing himself and was considered quite good at it. Pop was also a Justice of the Peace, and according to one story, he altered his birth certificate to take ten years off his age because he felt he was too young to retire.

Mouat's also bought logs from loggers and eggs and farm produce from farmers, much of which they exchanged for store-bought goods.

The store stayed open until 8:00 p.m. on Saturdays, but was closed on Sundays and on Wednesdays afternoons.

From the outside, the building looked much like it does today. The inside was a different matter:

- The post office was on the lower floor at the back of the store.

- The loading dock was at the back. Mouat's delivery truck would back up to it to load groceries for delivery to people's houses. Some of us kids would vie to go along for the ride, sitting nestled in with the boxes and sacks at the tailgate of the pickup truck.

- Auntie Maggie Manson, Jane Mouat's sister, lived on the upper floor, at the back of the building.

- Where the Volume Two bookstore, Pegasus Gallery, and La Cucina café are today is where the feed shed was. That's also where they candled eggs and cut glass to size for windows.

- The offices were upstairs. There was a wide, open staircase at the centre of the store. Gilbert Mouat would get up to his office via a hand-operated rope platform lift, which was behind the stairs.

Boat days were special days. Three days a week the *Princess Mary* of the CPR's coastal service arrived here from Vancouver, and the dock, as well as Mouat's store, were a hive of activity. At the sound of the ship's whistle, Bill Page or another Mouat's employee would come out from the feed shed to help it dock. While he was busy pulling in and securing the bow line, we kids would be waiting on the narrow portion of the dock behind the freight shed (where the Coast Guard offices are now) for a crew member to throw us its rear heaving line.

The first person to meet the boat was always the postmaster, "Pop" Eaton, who grabbed the mail bags and hustled up to the post office to start sorting. Some people would wait around for their mail or do their shopping or other errands and then come back.

## Boat Day Over the Years

Bob Rush's description of boat day certainly captures the feeling that would have existed in earlier days when the long-awaited boat arrived in Ganges Harbour, as well as in many other communities along the BC coast. Here's how E. R. Cartwright described (in his book *A Late Summer*) boat day when the SS *Iroquois* arrived in 1907: "On boat days we congregated at Ganges Wharf to meet the boat, supposedly to get the mail, but actually on the chance of getting the purser of SS *Iroquois* to relent, to open the bar and let us have a drink. The said purser, when he was feeling his best, might even be persuaded to part with a bottle of whiskey."

Whether it was mail, ice cream, whiskey, produce, livestock, visitors, or just the mystery of the unknown, boat day was an important part of people's lives, and Mouat's, with its dockside location, has always been right in the centre of things.

The top photo shows Ganges in about 1907, when Mouat's first bought the original Malcolm and Purvis store. The photo at the bottom shows Ganges in about 1945.

## Cowichan Sweaters

Ivan Mouat remembered that Mouat's bought Cowichan sweaters from Coast Salish people in the 1930s: "I remember when they [First Nations people] used to come and sell sweaters. They'd come in canoes with a great load of sweaters to sell to my Uncle Gilbert."

**The *Princess Mary*.** The *Princess Mary* was built in 1910 to travel from Victoria to Nanaimo and Comox, replacing smaller ships like the *Joan* and the *City of Nanaimo*. This steamer was 210 feet (64 m) long, weighed 1,700 tons, and had 59 first-class cabins (118 berths) and 30 second-class berths. She sailed the Strait of Georgia for the next forty years and, from 1932 to 1951, she served the Gulf Islands. According to Salt Spring resident Joane Millner, she made the eight-hour trip from Vancouver four days a week: "[It had] the full service, dining-room service, with napkins, finger bowls, all the trimmings. For a dollar, you could have a stateroom. Or for five dollars, you could have the bridal suite."

Crates of farm produce, butter, and livestock were on hand for shipment out. Visitors came off the boat, and freight of all kinds, such as sacks of feed and different grains would be trucked off the *Princess Mary* on hand carts. Grains would be placed directly into Mouat's feed shed, piled high in separate rows for each kind.

To us kids, one of the main things that the boat meant was that Mouat's ice cream counter would be re-stocked. The ice cream counter was just inside the front doors, to the left. If we were lucky, Colin Mouat ("Coddy") would be on duty at the ice cream counter. He was the one who was the most generous with the amount of ice cream he would put onto a cone.

If we were really lucky, a certain individual would be arriving back from a trip to the "big city." He would invariably be inebriated, but he enjoyed treating us kids to ice cream cones, which we were only too happy to encourage.

The ice cream came in padded ten-gallon containers, with a pouch of carbon dioxide crystals enclosed at the top to keep the ice cream frozen. After the *Princess Mary* left, we kids would take those pouches down to the dock and throw them in the water to watch the bubbles boil up. Ice cream wasn't sold in the grocery department to take home. Houses didn't have refrigerators, or if they did, refrigerators didn't have freezer compartments in those days.

## Financing the Store and Its Customers

As early as 1911, Mouat's financed itself by issuing shares (700 shares, each valued at $100, for a total of $70,000). Most of the shares were owned by family members, who traded them amongst themselves. However, some were owned by a very few, long-time employees like Ken Butterfield (accounts), Bill Page (manager of the feed shed), and Walter Norton (groceries and hardware). Although financing a business like this in a farming community was never easy, Peggy Johnston, the youngest of Gilbert's six children, remembers that shareholders always received an annual dividend on their shares.

**Mouat's share certificate.**
This share certificate was issued at the end of 1945 to William J. Mouat (Gilbert's son, Bill, who became a school superintendent in Abbotsford and eventually had a secondary school named after him).

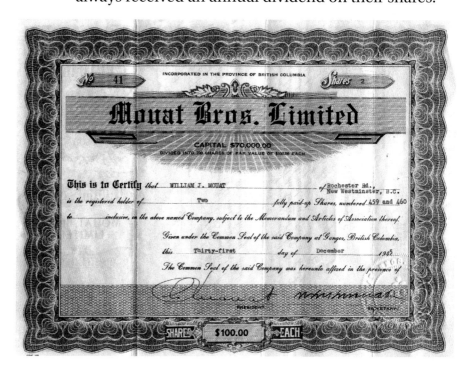

Customers, too, had to be financed. In some ways, Mouat's functioned like a company store, if you think of the island as the company. Islanders often had no money until they could sell the things they produced – fruit, vegetables, eggs, lambs and other animals, logs and lumber, and so on – so they bought the goods they needed from the store on credit. When their produce was ready to market, they brought it to the store to sell

**Bill Page and Cyril Wagg at Mouat's Feed Shed, c. 1920.**
Bill Page was the manager of Mouat's Feed Shed and a long-time company employee. He was one of only a few company employees to own Mouat's shares. Dick Toynbee remembered that employees played "some awful tricks" on Bill. For example, they would pile up junk in his office so he couldn't get in the door, and sometimes they would hide one of the bags of feed. This tortured Bill because he kept careful track of everything in the shed and liked to have each article in its correct place.

and applied what they received for the produce to the bills they had accumulated. Mouat's would then have to sell the goods it had received to others to pay its own bills. Little money actually changed hands between shopkeeper and customers.

In many cases, collecting from customers was very difficult, if not impossible. Here are two of Ivan Mouat's humorous accounts of this problem:

> Percy had a "chicken ranch," which was not a great producer, perhaps because Percy avoided work of any kind with great success. He owed Mouat's a lot of money, and one day my Uncle Gilbert decided it was time to bring the matter of Percy's indebtedness to his attention. Percy's response was, "Well Gilbert, I can't help it if my chickens don't lay!" That was just too much for Uncle Gilbert, who replied, "*Your* chickens? *Your* chickens? They surely must be *my* chickens. I've been feeding them for the last fifteen years!" This was too much for Percy, and he went off to obtain solace at the Harbour House pub. Evidently he got it, for he returned to the store an hour or so later with a burlap sack and let loose four white hens. "If they're your chickens, Gilbert, here they are!"

> In the early 1930s, the "Major" [Ivan never told us his real name] came out from England to Salt Spring Island. He had a grand time as an unattached young "man about the town." He later got married and had children – lots of children – and was no longer able to make ends meet. My father, W. M. Mouat, noticed that he had not paid his January, February, or March accounts – and it was almost the end of April. So Dad thought he should have a "word" with the Major about this situation. "Major, I notice you haven't paid your bill for some months and I was wondering if there was a problem?" "Well, yes, Willie, you know with all these children needing clothes and boots and so on, what I do is put the names of all my creditors in a box each month and pull out a name and pay each one until I have no money left. And dash it Willie, if I have any more of your cheek, I won't even put Mouat's name in the box!"

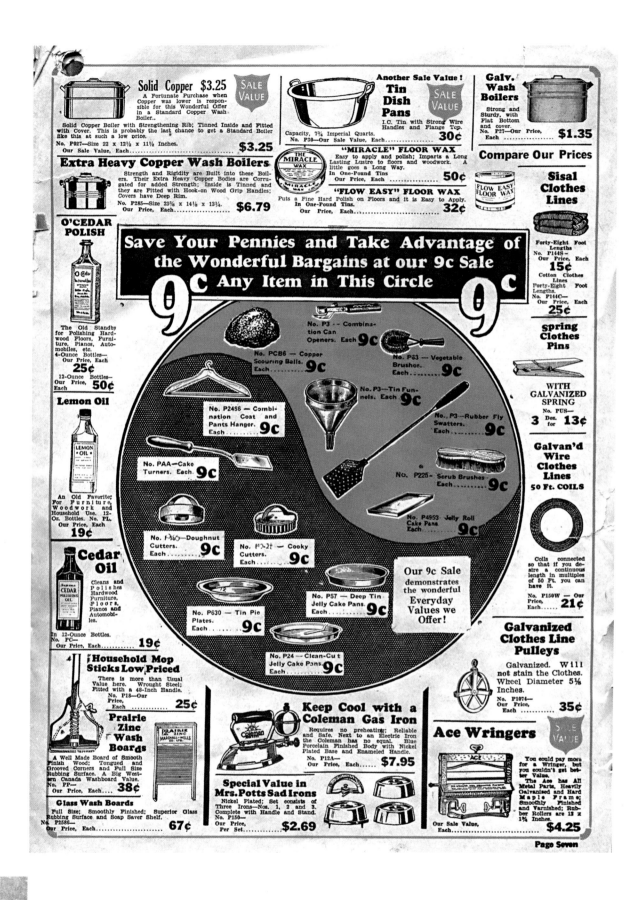

**William Manson Mouat (centre) with a young Jean Chrétien (left) and Liberal riding association president Mladen Zorkin (right).** W. M. was often in the shadow of his younger brothers, Gilbert and Gavin, who were more forceful businessmen.

While the store's survival was always W. M.'s first concern, he was also a charter member of the Lady Minto Hospital Board, a school trustee for many years, a justice of the peace, one of the pioneers of the chamber of commerce, and a pillar of the United Church. In later life, he was addicted to golf and bridge and continued as a passionate Liberal, often corresponding with Ottawa politicians and enthusiastically supporting them in British Columbia.

*Photo courtesy of Sue Mouat*

*Opposite:* **Page from 1934 Mouat's catalogue.** Mouat's was affiliated with Marshall-Wells. The prices shown on this page of the midsummer catalogue were "for cash only."

On his ninetieth birthday in 1974, W. M. was still lobbying for some of the things he had been wanting for years:

• The Fulford ferry terminal should be moved to Isabella Point.

• Ganges should be incorporated as a village.

• Mouat's should install an elevator.

# A Variety of Interests

Mouat's has always consisted of more than one building and more than one business. Almost right from the beginning, Mouat's included not only the store but also part of the original homestead and slaughterhouse on Tripp Road, which was run by Cecil Springford and Bob (R. J.) Wood. In Ganges, there was a garage, a gas station, a lumberyard, and a large feed shed beside the store, which was later converted into Mouat's Mall.

Mouat's also sold insurance and real estate. Percy Purvis had become the Salt Spring agent for the Norwich Fire Insurance Company of London, England, and Gilbert continued this business. Meanwhile, Arthur Inglis and Douglas Harris had established similar businesses. In 1928, they decided to combine forces.

**Granny's Boarding House, c. 1917.** Once the "new" building was completed in 1912, the old building became Jane Mouat's boarding house and later the Ganges Inn. Over the years this building housed the offices of a number of different businesses, including Salt Spring Lands.

The resulting company was called Salt Spring Lands and Investment Co. Ltd. (later shortened to Salt Spring Lands Ltd.). The original shareholders were Douglas Harris (the original manager of the Salt Spring Island Trading Company), Arthur Inglis, and Gilbert, William M., and Gavin Mouat. Harry Wright Bullock became a shareholder when the company was incorporated. Harris was the president, Gilbert the vice-president, and Inglis the secretary-treasurer.

**Gavin Mouat admiring one of Alfred Ruckle's antique guns.** Gavin sold his shares in Mouat's at about the same time as Salt Spring Lands was born. Throughout the Depression and the Second World War, he concentrated his energy on his Mountain Park Farm and the original Lady Minto Hospital.

After the war, Gavin took over Salt Spring Lands and built up a large business in timber brokerage and real estate. Gavin was also heavily involved in many community projects, including consolidating the island's small schools, bringing electricity to Salt Spring, reorganizing the Ganges Water Company into the North Salt Spring Waterworks, running the Gulf Islands Ferry Company, donating the land for the current Lady Minto Hospital, and creating Mouat Park.

In 1946, after his brother Gilbert's death, Gavin Mouat bought out most of the outstanding shares of Salt Spring Lands and became president and managing director. Gavin developed the company in a number of ways, as Jack Green, a company shareholder and employee, described it in 1954:

> At that time Salt Spring Lands operated out of the basement of the Ganges Inn. It was a mixed operation, handling insurance, real estate, subdivisions, log brokerage, trust funds, mortgages and financing, and, once in a while, auctions. In the same office were the North Salt Spring Waterworks and the Gulf Islands Ferry Company, both substantially Gavin Mouat projects. In the middle of it all Charlie Mellish had a desk where he repaired clocks and watches. If a tiny jewel flipped out of a watch that Charlie was working on, half the staff would crawl around with their noses to the floor until it was found.

# The Middle Years, 1946–1969

Ganges was still a quiet little village when Joane Millner arrived in 1946. Here is how she described it in a 1984 interview:

> It was so very, very different today to what it was in '46. To begin with, in the village there was no park. There was no fire department as such....There was no land behind the present firehall. There was no bank....

> There was just a causeway from the Trading Company to Mouat's....Coffins were supplied by Mouat's store and trucks were used as a hearse serviced by volunteers. The old hospital had a morgue service, serviced again by volunteers.

> The stores really were interesting. Where the hardware department is now [in Mouat's] was the grocery department and it had big stairs going up to the upper floor, wide stairs. And they had an office up there, which took care of all the money that was taken in on trolleys that went up to the office.

*Opposite*: **Ganges, c. 1940.** This photo clearly shows that Mouat's was located on "the peninsula," joined to the rest of the village by only a narrow causeway. That's Grace Point (named after Thomas and Jane Mouat's youngest child who died shortly after her father) on the right, and, yes, that's ocean separating the peninsula from the main road and the Salt Spring Island Trading Company just visible on the other side of the road.

In the diagram below the photo, Ivan Mouat identified all of the buildings. At this time, Mouat's buildings included the store, the Ganges Inn, the feed shed, the butcher shop (formerly Aunt Maggie's cottage), the power house, the workshop, and the garage run by Arthur Elliot. Another tenant in the late 1940s was Bill Crawford, who had a shoemaking shop in one of the small buildings behind Mouat's store.

After Gilbert Mouat's death, three of his sons – Laurence ("Laurie"), Colin, and Malcolm ("Mac") – took over the management of the business. Colin and Mac had just returned from the war and now assisted Laurie, who had held the fort with his father and uncle during the war years.

In 1947, the company letterhead listed W. M. as president, long-time employee Walter Norton as vice-president, Laurie Mouat as treasurer and managing director, Ivan Mouat as secretary, and Colin Mouat as sales manager. However, Laurie, Colin, and Mac were effectively running the company.

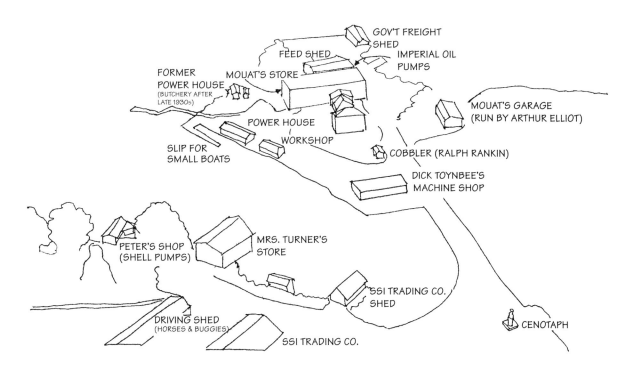

GOV'T FREIGHT SHED

FEED SHED

IMPERIAL OIL PUMPS

MOUAT'S STORE

FORMER POWER HOUSE (BUTCHERY AFTER LATE 1930s)

MOUAT'S GARAGE (RUN BY ARTHUR ELLIOT)

POWER HOUSE

WORKSHOP

COBBLER (RALPH RANKIN)

SLIP FOR SMALL BOATS

DICK TOYNBEE'S MACHINE SHOP

PETER'S SHOP (SHELL PUMPS)

MRS. TURNER'S STORE

SSI TRADING CO. SHED

CENOTAPH

DRIVING SHED (HORSES & BUGGIES)

SSI TRADING CO.

## Real Estate Initiatives

At the end of the 1940s, Mouat's built a new building beside the Ganges Inn, which was then rented to the Bank of Montreal from about 1950 to the mid-1960s. This arrangement worked very well for both parties until the bank bought the building from the company in 1966 for the grand sum of $30,000.

At about the same time, Mouat's negotiated the sale of six-tenths of an acre of land on the water at Grace Point to Imperial Oil for $50,000. Mouat's had been the Imperial Oil dealer for years, and the family's (if not the company's) involvement with Imperial Oil continued when Gavin Mouat's son, Norman, became the bulk-fuel agent for Esso in 1960.

**Anne and Colin Mouat (1979).**
"Colin was a person with remarkable drive, energy, and compassion. He was a favourite of Granny Mouat and spent his later teen years living primarily at the Ganges Inn and helping Granny as well as working in the store. He was interested in the church and liked working with young people. He was always available if any family member or anyone else needed a hand."

*From a memoir by Peggy Johnston, Gilbert's youngest child*

## Laurie Mouat

Laurie Mouat, the oldest of Gilbert and Belle's children, learned from an early age to work hard and to assume responsibility for all his siblings and later his parents. Laurie had always been interested in the business and as a young lad worked in the store at every opportunity. When he returned from Columbia College at age seventeen, he joined the company, and for the next forty-four years his ability, integrity, energy, and loyalty were dedicated to keeping this many-faceted business in sound condition by giving the best service to its customers and the community. He became the backbone of the family and of the business. Mouat Bros. was for Laurie, as it had been for his father and also his younger brother Mac, a lifetime vocation. Laurie's wife, Isabella, also worked in the store managing the dry goods and china departments for seventeen years before retiring.

*From a memoir by Peggy Johnston with additional material supplied by Vonnie Bryant.*

Photo courtesy of Vonnie Bryant

Mac (left) and Laurie Mouat in front of Mouat's office counter in the late-1960s

While the merchandizing end of the business held its own, the real estate side boomed. The company's annual report for 1959 enthusiastically chronicles land deals – construction of the new Island Garage (rented to Bill Trelford) on fill, the sale of a lot from the company's farm property on St. Mary Lake (Tripp Road), negotiations for the land sale to Imperial Oil, and the demolition of the Ganges Inn to make way for a new office building, which would house Salt Spring Lands and others.

## Mac Mouat

Mac Mouat, the youngest son of Gilbert and Belle Mouat, grew up within the store environment and related family businesses. With his brother Laurie, he had worked in the store for many years before taking over the co-management of the business after Gilbert's death in 1946. Mac had just returned from serving in the Canadian artillery during the war.

Like Laurie, Mac was a quiet and unassuming man, carrying on the business with his father's strong work ethic, his integrity in business dealings, and his concern for and responsibility to the shareholders. Mac brought to the business, among other things, his aptitude with working with numbers and his likeability.

Mac and Laurie were both avid fishermen, keeping separate boats moored at a dock behind the store and enjoying a friendly rivalry over their fishing triumphs. Mac had also been a keen soccer player in his youth and, along with his uncle W. M., was a founding member of the Salt Spring Island Golf Club.

When Mouat's was sold in 1969, Mac bought the Imperial Oil Bulk Plant and Fuel Dock Agency in Ganges from his cousin Norman Mouat and managed it until 1974, when he sold it to his daughter and son-in-law, Laurie and Bruce Fiander.

*From a memoir by Peggy Johnston with additional material supplied by Daphne Mouat and Laurie Fiander*

Photo courtesy of Carolyn Mouat

Imperial Oil Bulk Plant managers and workers (from left to right) Bruce Fiander, Dan Akerman, and Mac Mouat

## The Fifties

As their sister Peggy Johnston recounts, "As the years went on, Mac and Laurie assumed the running of the business. They worked very closely together and both continued to work very hard through good and somewhat difficult years."

The early fifties were difficult for almost everyone on Salt Spring as transportation services such as the CPR service from Vancouver were cut, banks were cautious about lending money to islanders, logging was in decline, farming was marginal, and people started moving away to try to find work. Everyone in the Mouats' extended family pitched in to keep the business going.

While practices often change more slowly in a small community, even a relatively isolated island

**Ganges Inn, c. 1937.** Granny's Boarding House (aka the Ganges Inn) was expanded and changed in the 1930s. After Jane, the inn was managed first by a Mr. and Mrs. Foe and later by Evelyn and Cecil Baker. It was taken over by Henry McGill in 1946 and run as a hotel until McGill opened a bakery there. Rooms were rented out for office space, including Salt Spring Lands, the provincial assessor's office, the public health nurse, and the school board offices. The building was taken down in 1959 and a new building constructed for Salt Spring Lands on part of the lot.

Photo by Derrick Lundy, courtesy of the Gulf Islands Driftwood

## Delivering the Goods

From its beginnings and to the present day Mouat's has delivered large purchases to its customers. From the mid-1950s to the mid-1980s, the company hired Dick Royal (R. S. Royal Trucking) to make many of these deliveries, as well as off-island pick-ups. Dick became a well respected and highly valued part of Mouat's operations and was considered one of the family.

community is affected by changes beyond its shores. In the fifties, this was the case for Mouat's as well as for its customers. As an example, before the war, customers were given up to ninety days to pay their accounts at the store. After the war, the ninety-day period was reduced to thirty.

Even today, in a small community like Salt Spring (with a 2006 population of about 10,000, but only about 2,000 in 1951), the market is often too small to support many competitors. Stores like Mouat's must make careful decisions about the goods and services they are going to offer. Probably for this reason, Mouat's gave up its garage in the fall of 1952, as this was a specialized area that others were able to do better.

Colin Mouat left the company in 1956 to join his uncle, Gavin Mouat, in Salt Spring Lands. His brothers Mac and Laurie continued to run the company, maintaining the friendly ambiance that has always been an important part of the working environment. Marguerite Lee, who worked weekends, holidays, and summers for Mouat's as a young girl from 1957 to about 1962, remembers that everyone referred to those involved in Mouat's management as "Uncle so and so" or "Aunt so and so." So, for example, general manager Laurie Mouat was Uncle Laurie, and his wife was Aunt Isabelle (her real name is Isabella). Marguerite remembers the Mouat's management and staff as being much older than is common today.

## Employer-Employee Relations

In 1957, the atmosphere around Mouat's was strained when there was talk of an employees' union. Laurie and Mac felt strongly that a union would destroy the small-town feeling that Mouat's had always had. They discussed things thoroughly with their employees, who ended up agreeing with them.

The union idea was dropped, and Mouat's returned to the family environment that had existed for years. Laurence Cartwright, who worked for the company during the 1950s, was very complimentary to Laurie Mouat's approach to staff:

> I think Uncle Laurie was the right man at the right time and I can never once recall him reprimanding anyone in front of others. In fact, he was very diplomatic and he had the personality that I am sure made people want to try a little harder. I can recall him coming to me one Saturday. I was loading a truck for somewhere and in a cheerful way he said, "Laurence, you have got to stop having accidents. Our insurance is going sky high." I think anyone else, and with good reason, would have laid down the law to me, but it was this manner that I have tried to follow as much as possible. Results can be obtained, and he knew how.

**Ganges, 1956.** In the fifties, Ganges still looked like a sleepy village. The Bank of Montreal in the centre of the photo opened in 1950 near its current location. Both the bank and the Esso station across from Mouat's, where the Grace Point development is today, were on the shore, as there had not yet been any landfill.

Under Mac and Laurie, Mouat's was a place that protected its employees and lived with their various idiosyncrasies. Most of the staff had been with the company for many years. This familial approach to employment was neighbourly and humane, if not always practical.

**Mouat's grocery store**. Mouat's sold groceries in the store's basement during the 1950s and 1960s. This grocery department was run by Ben Greenhough for many years, until, in about 1965, Mouat's gave up the grocery part of its business, leasing the premises (shown here) to Ben and his son of the same name, who called their new grocery Bens' Lucky Dollar Store. At one time, there was a small tunnel from Henry McGill's bakery in the Ganges Inn to the grocery store. Like the store itself, the tunnel was occasionally flooded when the tide was exceptionally high and the wind strong, a problem that persists in Mouat's basement, to a much lesser extent, today.

# Changes in Ganges

**Ganges, 1960.** Compare this view with the one twenty years earlier on page 31. Mouat's is still located on a peninsula, but one that has been extended. More of the land has been cleared, and there are more buildings, as well as new bulk fuel storage containers. The Ganges Inn has been replaced by a new building housing Salt Spring Lands.

Mouat's grocery and butcher departments moved downstairs after the war, and Ben Greenhough managed these departments in the fifties and sixties. Ben, his wife, Merlie, and their two sons lived in the suite at the top of the Mouat's building during much of that time. (Earlier and at different times, both Colin and Mac Mouat, among others, had lived there.)

*Photo by A. Marshall Sharp*

**Ganges, 1960.** This photo shows the newly filled area across from the Salt Spring Island Trading Company where the Ganges firehall now stands. The Mouat buildings are still on the small peninsula, but the surrounding area is growing. The piles of lumber to the left of the Salt Spring Island Trading Company represent Mouat's lumberyard at this time. The *Motor Princess* (on the left) continued to dock at Ganges until 1963.

*Photo by A. Marshall Sharp*

*Photos courtesy of Gil Mouat*

**Bill Trelford's garage at Grace Point and the barber shop on the other side of the parking lot.** These are both shown in the photo at the top of this page.

*Photo by A. Marshall Sharp*

**Ganges, c. 1960.** From this angle – a ground-level view – Ganges is beginning to look more like it looks today.

# The Sixties

Mouat's was a community institution right from the beginning, and this pattern continued during the sixties. It provided credit to those who couldn't afford to buy what they needed and did what it could to help those in need. When the new library association required space, Mouat's provided a room in the store for a nominal rent so that the Centennial Library could open its doors in 1959.

Although salaries at Mouat's were not as high as those in the public sector, there were many extras – Christmas bonuses, staff discounts, and other perks. Mouat's gave jobs to individuals who might not have been able to find work elsewhere, as well as to young people who needed jobs. The latter worked on their Christmas and Easter holidays, on weekends, and during the summers.

The sixties were characterized by many changes. While Mouat's still sold clothes and shoes, fabric,

Photo by A. Marshall Sharp

**Ganges, 1967.** Compare this photo with the one on page 31. The largest areas of the harbour that have been filled to this point include what is now Centennial Park and the fire hall across from it. Mouat's peninsula has grown too.

ice cream, hardware, building materials, and more, it had stopped selling groceries and feed (Buckerfield's now leased an area from Mouat's for a feed shed managed by Ted Gear), and it no longer had its own garage. These changes helped the company concentrate on the areas in which it was strongest, and thus become more profitable. One of these areas was lumber, which was always a lucrative part of Mouat's business.

Mouat's remained a large landowner, and rentals formed an important part of its revenue. For example, Mouat's 1961 year-end statement contains the following "rentals schedule": four cottages, the post office, the BC Telephone Company, the island garage, the RCMP, Salt Spring Lands, the Bank of Montreal, a barber shop, a taxi stand, the Centennial Library, Buckerfields, and the Imperial Oil lease. The total rent collected for this property in 1960 amounted to $13,746.85. The company's lumber warehouse and wharf also provided revenue.

**The new shareholders, c. 1997.**
*From left to right:* Tom and Yvonne Toynbee, Dick and Barbara Toynbee, Manson Toynbee, Carolyn and Norman Mouat, and Halvor Eide (who became a shareholder in 1986). *Absent from photo:* shareholders John Lees (a friend of Dick's from Vancouver and Salt Spring) and Dave Miller (Dick's partner from his days with Miller and Toynbee Real Estate).

# The Modern Era, 1969–1999

By 1969, Laurie and Mac were ready to sell the business – preferably to someone in the family. Their cousin Dick Toynbee expressed an interest and, with others, soon bought the company.

With brothers Manson and Tom, Dick had grown up on Salt Spring Island. His father, Richard, had run the Ganges Garage from the 1920s until his untimely death at 57 in 1947. After graduating from UBC, Dick left the island, eventually settling in Terrace, BC, working in real estate. He returned to Salt Spring in the late 1960s to buy the family business.

When Dick purchased Mouat Bros. Co. Ltd., the company's shares were worth eight times their original value. The new company was called Mouat's Trading Co. Ltd.

Dick realized that if Mouat's and the village of Ganges were going to survive, they would have to expand and grow. There was pressure to relocate existing businesses, including food stores, banks, and the post office, to Upper Ganges or Central. Parking had always been a problem and would have to be provided somehow. Dick decided to solve this problem by filling in the mud flats between Mouat's and what had been Mrs. Turner's store (see page 31) and later the White Elephant restaurant. In his first busy year, Dick also purchased the Salt Spring Island Trading Company and its building, as well as the White Elephant restaurant building.

Dick brought in Spencer Marr, an accountant he knew from his days in Terrace, BC, to manage the store. He also hired Hank Schubart, the island's premier architect of the day, to come up with an

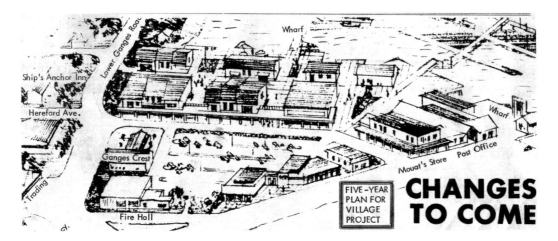

FIVE-YEAR
PLAN FOR
VILLAGE
PROJECT

# CHANGES TO COME

**New Mouat's complex**. This is what architect Hank Schubart envisioned in 1970 for the new Mouat's complex (as printed in the *Gulf Islands Driftwood*).

**Ganges, 1970**. This photo shows the large area that had been filled in. In 2006, it accommodated the Thrifty's, Harbour, and Ganges Centre buildings.

overall development plan for the area that would complement the existing buildngs. The foundation for the new company was now firmly in place.

A year and a half later, the company had filled the shallow backwater behind the fire hall in Ganges and had purchased The Ship's Anchor Inn (the historic building across the street from Thrifty's) and the foreshore rights extending across the bay to Mouat's store. The company was planning to construct a new store in the reclaimed area and to pave the new parking area. A sewage plant was also planned to take care of the needs of the new complex.

MOUAT'S: THE FIRST HUNDRED YEARS

# The Right Man for the Job

Dick didn't feel that he was particularly well suited to the role of general manager of Mouat's, and it was clear that strong, dynamic leadership was required for the company to prosper. Dick found that leadership in his younger brother, Tom.

In 1971, Tom Toynbee had no plans to return to Salt Spring, where he'd grown up. After graduating from UBC, he had established a career for himself in the lumber business in Vancouver and had a number of good career possibilities in the offing. Nevertheless, when Dick approached him, the excitement of the company's potential in Ganges intrigued him, and he decided to take the job.

**Dick Toynbee (left) with store manager Ian Brown in 1971.** Ian, who had considerable experience in managing hardware stores, was brought in from Calgary to replace Spencer Marr. This was about the same time that Tom Toynbee became general manager. Ian later became a shareholder in the company. Ian managed Mouat's from 1971 to 1989.

In 1971, Mouat's built a new building, the Harbour Building, on some of the landfill put in the year before. Ben Greenhough and his son moved their Bens' Lucky Dollar Store into the new building. However, by 1972, they decided to sell the business to K & R Food Store Ltd., which later became Ganges Village Market (GVM). Mike Tyson, who managed the K & R store for a year and a half, remembered that the building was like a big box and hadn't been properly designed for a grocery store. Some will remember the store's large, highly extroverted cat named Mr. In-Between.

**Inside of Bens' Lucky Dollar Store.** That's Ben, Sr., on the left and his wife, Merlie, in the centre.

**Ganges Village Market, c. 1987.** GVM's first location was on the waterfront – in the Harbour Building, which Mouat's constructed for Ben Greenhough and his son.

MOUAT'S: THE FIRST HUNDRED YEARS

This period of intensive development was financially difficult for Mouat's. To address the concerns of creditors, a plan was put together aimed at placing the company on a solid financial footing within a year. During this period, neither Dick nor Tom drew a salary. To save money, Dick did off-island trucking, and Tom doubled as a building materials salesman while managing all aspects of the company. Their survival during this period was facilitated by the incredible support they received from their wives, their brother Manson, who was pursuing a teaching career, and their cousin Norm Mouat and his wife Carolyn, all of whom were also company shareholders.

**Tom Toynbee celebrating Mouat's seventieth anniversary in 1977.**
In addition to heading up Mouat's, Tom spent many years as chairman of BC Buildings Corporation, was the main advocate and a tireless worker for the installation of a sewage treatment system in Ganges, and has served on the board of the Salt Spring Island Foundation for many years. As a student at UBC, Tom was captain of the eight-oar crew that won a gold medal at the 1954 British Empire Games.

## Disaster Strikes

"In April 1976, I was totally paralysed by Guillain-Barré syndrome [an acute disorder of the peripheral nerves causing weakness and often paralysis of the limbs]. Yvonne had to look after me and the family. We didn't know if or by how much I would recover. The decision to bring in Cubbon [see page 50] was, to a great degree, motivated by my uncertainty over my health."

*Tom Toynbee*

Photo courtesy of Carolyn Mouat

**Mouat and Toynbee women, Christmas, c. 1980.** *From left to right:* Barbara Toynbee, Carolyn Mouat, and Yvonne Toynbee and her daughter, Colleen Toynbee, all of whom were very involved in the business.

# False Alarms

After repeated burglaries, Mouat's installed an alarm system in the store in about 1980. When the alarm was tripped, store-manager Ian Brown was the first to be called to the store, followed by Dick and finally Tom. There they would meet the RCMP officer on duty. Fortunately, most of these turned out to be false alarms.

One night, Ian, Dick, and Tom arrived to hear a rookie policeman exploring the upstairs. All of a sudden, they heard him yell, "Freeze!" They hurried upstairs to find the young policeman nervously pointing his gun at a mannequin.

*Photo by A. Marshall Sharp*

**The Lady Minto Thrift Shop in Mouat's Mall, c. 1972.** Most of the shops in Mouat's basement were small and crowded like this one.

## Horses at the Store

Ian Brown, Mouat's store manager, remembered that, when he started at Mouat's, occasionally you might see a horse tied up at the front or rear of the store. The police only started discouraging the practice in 1971!

## More Changes

Mouat's had once been a real department store, selling just about everything and anything, and providing many services too. More and more, the store – or stores as was increasingly the case – became more specialized and rented space to tenants who provided products and services that Mouat's had once provided.

Mouat's always owned a fair bit of property in Ganges. The company had rented out garage space to mechanics like Richard Toynbee in the twenties and Arthur Elliot in the fifties. It had rented to the Bank of Montreal and had smaller buildings available for a barber shop, a cobbler, and accommodation for Mouat family members.

Beginning in the 1970s, the company started erecting larger buildings on its property to provide rental revenue. Bens' Lucky Dollar followed by the K & R grocery store in the Harbour Building were among the first tenants. When Mouat's basement was freed up, it was converted into a mall, which was rented out to small businesses.

**Others were also building**. The Bank of Montreal bought the building it had been renting from Mouat's in 1966. Just a few years later, the bank expanded the existing building into the larger structure it still owns today.

Photo by A. Marshall Sharp

Mouat's had from its very beginning contained a post office. The post office dated from the Malcolm and Purvis days when a general store was the logical place for this service. (Jane Mouat had been post-mistress from 1908 until her death in 1935.) However, by the 1970s, Mouat's was able to build a separate building to house an enlarged post office. The Purvis Building, built on the site formerly occupied by Salt Spring Lands, was erected for this purpose in 1971 and then rented to what is now Canada Post. (The post office is now in the Ganges Centre Building and is still one of Mouat's tenants.)

**The Purvis Building.** The toy store in the north end of the Purvis Building is the centre of a parade celebrating Mouat's 90th anniversary in 1997. The other end of the building currently houses an ice cream store.

Photo courtesy of Mouat's Trading Co. Ltd.

*Photo courtesy of Mouat's Trading Co. Ltd.*

**Dorothy Brown (left) in the Salty Shop.** As part of its growing specialization, Mouat's asked Dorothy to develop a separate "variety store" within the ground floor of the main store, and thus the Salty Shop was born in 1975. Dorothy's shop design included souvenirs, greeting cards, giftware, bulk candy, chocolates, film, magazines, cosmetics, candles, tobacco products, and more. The store was an immediate success. The Salty Shop moved into the Harbour Building almost fifteen years later.

In 1976, Mouat's formed a partnership with Cubbon Building Supplies and built a new building on its Rainbow Road property. Building supplies were then moved from the Mouat's building to the new Rainbow Road facility. This freed up the old waterfront feed shed, which was remodelled and attached to the main building to provide additional space for Mouat's Mall.

A significant change occurred in 1981 when Mouat's became associated with Home Hardware. For years, Mouat's had struggled to improve its buying power so that it could compete with larger retail outlets. Home Hardware, with its 1,100-member association, made this possible.

In 1982, Mouat's built the Ganges Centre Building at the south of the large shopping area to house the Canadian Imperial Bank of Commerce, Canada Post, and ultimately other offices and stores.

*Photo courtesy of Mouat's Trading Co. Ltd.*

**Ganges Centre Building nearing completion, 1982**

MOUAT'S: THE FIRST HUNDRED YEARS

Photo by Charles Kahn

**A Schubart design.** The Mouat's-Cubbon partnership was too small to become part of a strong buying group and obtain the discounts it needed to be competitive with larger companies. Competition with Windsor Plywood for a small market and the tough times of the recession in the early 1980s convinced Mouat's and Cubbon to get out of the building supply business.

In 1985, Mouat's sold the business, but not the building, to Windsor Plywood, which continued to rent the Rainbow Road building for a few years until Mouat's finally sold that too. Interestingly, the Rainbow Road building was originally designed by Hank Schubart, probably the only such commercial building in the prestigious architect's portfolio.

## Community Building

The Mouats and Toynbees have always been very community-minded. One of the most successful island endeavours got started in 1984, when Dick Toynbee, John Lees, Colin Mouat, and Alan Pierce founded the Salt Spring Island Foundation. The revenue from the Foundation's endowment fund annually supports a wide range of worthwhile community organizations. The Foundation gave out grants totalling more than $80,000 in 2005, just over twenty years after it was founded.

# Preparing for Further Expansion: The Ganges Sewer System

Salt Spring's official community plan specified that Ganges be the commercial and cultural centre of the island. However, until 1986, there was no sewage disposal system in the village, although sewage disposal had been a problem since the early 1960s. Of most concern were the hospital, which had an inadequate drainage system, and the Consolidated School, which discharged its sewage directly into Ganges Harbour. While some waterfront shops also discharged sewage directly into the ocean, many businesses stored sewage in tanks and trucked it to a disposal site on a nearby farm. However, the lack of a sewer system severely limited further development in Ganges.

**Ganges sewage treatment plant.** This plant (in the centre top of the photo) has been rated among the top three such plants in BC because of the purity of its outflow.

Photo courtesy of Mouat's Trading Co. Ltd.

MOUAT'S: THE FIRST HUNDRED YEARS

Photo by Charles Kahn

**The Jessie Toynbee buildings.**
In 2006, the building on the left, located on Lower Ganges Road, contained a floor covering store as its main tenant, while the one on the right housed a Sear's outlet, a physiotherapy clinic, an accountant, and a consignment clothing store.

Mouat's had proposed building a sewage system for its own use, but the provincial government refused to approve a system unless it served all of Ganges. Mouat's then started actively campaigning for a Ganges-wide system. Opponents of the system were concerned that the addition of a sewage system would promote further growth and development on the island. At the risk of alienating a significant portion of its clientele, Mouat's took a strong political position on the need for the sewer system. The ensuing struggle was protracted and bitter, but eventually the need for a sewage treatment plant overcame the opposition and a system was approved. Funding was arranged, construction began, and the sewer system was completed in 1986.

Once the sewer system was in place, Mouat's was able to build the second of the two Jessie Toynbee Buildings (named for Tom, Dick, and Manson's mother). The first was built to house the Island Savings Credit Union. It hadn't been possible to develop the second building until the sewer system existed because the land it was to be built on contained the Credit Union's septic field.

**Boardwalk Greens.** For almost a decade, the successive owners of this little shop between Mouat's main store and the Harbour Building have rented the space from Mouat's. The temporary building moved here by original owner Gloria O'Hara is now taking on a feeling of permanence, and the shop, which now sells plants and garden accessories, adds beauty to the Ganges core.

**Chamber of Commerce.** This building, fronting on Lower Ganges Road, was rebuilt in 1990 and continues to house the Salt Spring Chamber of Commerce and the tourist information centre.

The new sewer system allowed the development of Ganges to continue along the waterfront. It also ensured that buildings like ArtSpring, the Gulf Islands Secondary School, and Creekside could be built.

*Photo by Charles Kahn*

*Photo by Charles Kahn*

MOUAT'S: THE FIRST HUNDRED YEARS

**Thrifty's Building** *(top).* The last of Mouat's buildings was constructed in 1992 to house Thrifty Foods.

**Salt Spring Island Trading Company Building (bottom).** Mouat's renovated this building in 1994, winning the Renovation of the Year Award from the Victoria Real Estate Board in the process.

*Photo by Charles Kahn*

*Photo by Charles Kahn*

**Mary Paul (left) and Barb Isles with their creation – Mouat's Clothing**

## Clothing Specialists

Barb Isles had designed successful clothing stores in Ontario for years; Mary Paul had been a buyer of women's clothing and a store manager. When they found themselves on Salt Spring, they decided to open a clothing shop here. In their search for the perfect location, they soon met Tom Toynbee, since Mouat's owned the best rental property in Ganges. Tom convinced them to form a partnership with Mouat's, and, as they say, the rest is history.

Barbara Toynbee had run the clothing department in Mouat's store from 1969. She was pleased to retire in 1988 and leave the designing and managing of the new store – Mouat's Clothing – to Barb and Mary. When they were finished, Mouat's had moved from gumboots to chic (although gumboots are still for sale) and today has a destination clothing store as part of its retail operations.

## Old Salty

Mary Lou Bompas, who began working in Old Salty (formerly the Salty Shop) with Dorothy Brown in 1982, took over as manager of the shop when Dorothy retired in 1989. Old Salty, which currently shares the front of the Harbour Building with Mouat's Clothing, was redesigned in 1999 by Barb Isles and Mary Lou. It has been a great success and now stocks a variety of quality items that appeal to both locals and tourists, including BC hand-crafted jewellery, Canadian Native art, and Salt Spring Island luxury bath and wellness products.

**Spicing up Old Salty**. 1980s manager Ian Brown remembered that "with her sense of humour and expertise, Mary Lou Bompas added a lot to the Salty Shop." Above Suzanne Jackson (left) and Mary Lou model a pair of intriguing T-shirts, only one of many imaginative outfits Mary Lou has worn in her 25 years in the shop. The photos to the right were supplied by Ian Brown.

**Main store co-managers David Griffiths and Kim Young**

## Home Hardware, The Housewares Store, and Bed, Bath, and Homeware

Home Hardware, The Housewares Store, and Bed, Bath, and Homeware occupy the original Mouat's building. The stores are co-managed by David Griffiths and Kim Young and remain true to the company's past while adopting fresh ideas. As Belle Mouat said of the original Mouat's, "You'll go some to find a store in the city that looks better than this."

**Winning.** Mary Paul, Barb Isles, then store manager Halvor Eide, Mary Lou Bompas, and Vicki Christensen pose with the Home Award for Merchandising Excellence, which the store won in 1991.

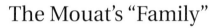

**Manson Toynbee and his mother, Jessie Mouat Toynbee, serving up cake at Mouat's 85th anniversary, 1992**

## The Mouat's "Family"

Here are a few photographic memories of some of Mouat's fantastic staff who have functioned much like a big, happy family. They have celebrated business triumphs, personal events like birthdays, seasonal delights like summer (picnics) and Christmas (parties), and often Mouat's milestones.

**Mouat's 90th anniversary, 1997.** Among the many familiar faces celebrating is Ivan Mouat partially hidden on the left.

**Best wishes, Carole.** Wendy Newton (main store manager, 2002–2005), Carole Coburn, Ben Martens (main store manager, 1994–2002), Ali Kerr (office manager since 2001), Gaye Ferguson, and Mary Lou Bompas wish Carole well at her going-away party in September 1992. It's a Mouat's tradition to have parties for departing employees.

**The Mouat's team at the company's 90th anniversary in 1997.** *(left to right) back row:* Wendy Newton, Yvonne Akerman, Woody Ensminger, Suzanne Jackson, Dale Howell, Lydia Turner, Lynda Sims, Tom Toynbee, Andrew Watt, Chad Kinnear; *third row:* Edie Fishloch, Jen Ferrier, Steven Martens, Keith Newman, Ben Martens, Heather Kusch, Yvonne Sollitt, Ali Kerr, Kim Mailey; *second row:* Barb Isles, Treva Hinchcliff, Barry Hayne, Mary Lou Bompas, Elaine Dunster, Beverley Wells, Marie-Clair Garner, Dawn Sawchuck, Jane Hamilton, Kim Young; *front row:* Mary Paul, Nadine Gordon, Elaine Beathe, Cheryl Johnson, Barb Kinnear, Sara Wasic, Gordie Alton, Brian Kerr.

## Completing the First Hundred Years, 1999–2007

In 1999, when Tom Toynbee decided to retire, the company shareholders agreed that they would prefer to sell the company to someone connected to the family. Mouat's was bought by a new group of people consisting mainly of Dick Toynbee's son-in-law Kevin Bell (now Mouat's president and general manager), his four brothers, and their spouses. The new owners included Kevin and Nicola Bell, Pat and Dolores Bell, Gerry and Kelly Bell, Michael and Darlene Bell, Dan and Joanne Bell, Ken Almond, and Dianne Almond. Richard Toynbee, Jr., and Tom and Yvonne Toynbee continued as shareholders in the new company.

**Kevin Bell at work in his Mouat's office.** Kevin Bell first came to Salt Spring in 1971 when he was a student at the University of Victoria. He met Nicola Toynbee (Dick and Barbara's daughter) in the same year, and they married in 1973. Kevin worked for Gulf Oil for a couple of years in Calgary before retraining to work in real estate. He joined Miller and Toynbee Real Estate on Salt Spring and worked as a notary as well as a real estate and insurance agent until 1988, when he moved to Victoria. He returned to Salt Spring in 1999 once his three children had completed university.

*Photo by Charles Kahn*

La Cucina Italian Grill
in Mouat's mall

Having taken over a well-run company from Tom Toynbee, Kevin has concentrated on improving the firm's retail operations, with a focus on extensive building renovations. This involved a complete makeover of Home Hardware in 2002 and 2003, as well as Mouat's Clothing and Old Salty in 2006, all under the direction of Barb Isles.

Retaining top-notch staff is another of Kevin's priorities. While it's difficult for retail businesses to compete with the level of remuneration provided in public sector jobs like the government or in Crown corporations like BC Ferries, Mouat's has long had a profit-sharing program, which gives employees a real stake in the company, much as shareholding did for some employees in the past.

**The Oystercatcher Seafood Bar and Grill on the second level of the Harbour Building is located above Shipstones Tap Room and Lounge.** Co-owner Barry Kazakoff continuously fine-tunes each of his restaurants and its image.

Kevin's era has also seen the company branch out into the restaurant business through a partnership with restaurateur Barry Kazakoff in The Oystercatcher Seafood Bar & Grill, La Cucina Italian Grill, and Shipstones Tap Room and Lounge. All these restaurants rent space from Mouat's.

MOUAT'S: THE FIRST HUNDRED YEARS

Photo by Charles Kahn

**Aunt Maggie's Cottage (now the home of the Tree House Cafe), Ganges.** Set in a gardenlike atmosphere between Mouat's Clothing, Old Salty, and Mouat's Hardware, the Tree House Cafe, with its entertainment and informal ambiance, draws people to the area, particularly in the summer months.

The rental of Aunt Maggie Manson's old cottage between Mouat's hardware and Old Salty to Tree House Cafe has combined with the three Mouat's restaurants to make the area a hive of activity. Locals and visitors alike are attracted by the variety of appealing shops and restaurants (some with live entertainment).

**Moby's Marine Pub.** When Moby's closed its doors in the spring of 2005, islanders went into a brief period of mourning. The rumour mill soon announced that it would reopen, and reopen it did, thanks to the partnership of Barry Kazakoff and Kevin Bell of Mouat's. This fourth addition to the partnership is the only one located in a building not owned by Mouat's.

Photo by Charles Kahn

## Now, that's trust!

In a bad snow storm in January 2005, I went into Mouat's to buy a couple of tanks for my propane lamp. Despite being cold and dimly lit, with no operating sales system, and with only a single employee, Mouat's was open for business.

Many other islanders had struggled in to purchase items they required, and they weren't disappointed. The lonely clerk instructed the customers to take what they needed, to leave their names and telephone numbers behind, and to come back when the weather improved to settle up. As it turned out, all those thankful customers eventually paid for their purchases.

*Gundy McLeod*

From its inception in 1907 to the present time, Mouat's has remained an important player in the development of Ganges as a delightful seaside village. Mouat's owns and operates five retail businesses (Home Hardware; the Housewares Store; Bed, Bath, and Homeware; Old Salty; and Mouat's Clothing). It co-owns four restaurants (The Oystercatcher, La Cucina, Shipstones Pub, and Moby's). It is also the landlord for thirty-two businesses in the heart of the village. And perhaps most importantly, staff report that Mouat's is still a great place to work.

**Mouat's staff, 2006:** Gordy Alton, Thomas Baker, Lorne Bascom, Kevin Bell, Mary Lou Bompas, Ajada Cambridge, Megan Caron, Darin Craig, Devon Craig, Penny Dale, Katie Drummond, Elaine Dunster, Gordy Fergusson, Debra Fletcher, Erin Foster, Kate Gooding, Nadine Gordon, David Griffiths, Deb Hamilton, Mattie Hammond, Barry Hayne, Elaine Head, Ann Heggeler, Cassie Heggeler, Treva Hinchcliffe, Dale Howell, Barb Isles, Geoff Ison, Alison Kerr, Charles Kinch, Barb Kinnear, Barb Layard, Fiona Longeau, Alisha Matherne, Jeremiah Mathis, Jacquelin Midget, Mary Paul, Matt Ripley, Jennifer Schmelzle, Angela Schult, Sue Schult, Brooke Shergold, Carol Siemko, Anna Squier, Devon Underwood, Reynaard Vergalen, Bev Wells, Carol Wenger, Cherie Worsley, Debbie Wrate, Kim Young

Photo by John Cameron, NewBasics, courtesy of Mouat's Trading Co. Ltd.

MOUAT'S: THE FIRST HUNDRED YEARS

63

The author would like to thank the following people for providing material, information, or ideas that have been used in this book: Dennis Beech, Kevin Bell, Mary Lou Bompas, Ian Brown, Vonnie Bryant, Vicki Christensen, Brenda Eaton, Halvor Eide, Bruce and Laurie Fiander, Ben Greenhough, Natalie Horel (for the quotations by Charlie Horel), Barb Isles, Peggy Johnston, Ali Kerr, Marguerite Lee, Ben Martens, Anne Mouat, Carolyn Mouat, Daphne Mouat, Gil Mouat, Mac Mouat, Sue Mouat, Frank Neumann and the Salt Spring Island Archives, Wendy Newton, Judy Norget, Mary Paul, Lotus Ruckle, Bob Rush, Ian Shopland, Gail Sjuberg and the *Gulf Islands Driftwood*, Barbara Toynbee, Tom Toynbee, Mike Tyson.

**Library and Archives Canada Cataloguing in Publication**

Kahn, Charles, date
    Mouat's : the first hundred years / Charles Kahn.

ISBN 0-9739990-0-4

1. Mouat's Trading Company--History. 2. General stores-- British Columbia--Saltspring Island--History. 3. Stores, Retail-- British Columbia—Saltspring Island--History. I. Mouat's Trading Company II. Title.

HF5465.C34M68 2006    381'.1'0971128    C2006-900060-3

*Conception, text, and picture research:* Charles Kahn
*Design and layout:* Mark Hand
*Photo credits:* All photos courtesy of Salt Spring Island Archives unless otherwise noted.
*Printing:* Friesens